FIVE 5 FINGER PIANO

POP HITS

ISBN 978-1-4803-6187-4

HAL•LEONARD®
CORPORATION

7777 W. BLUEMOUND RD. P.O. BOX 13819 MILWAUKEE, WI 53213

Visit Hal Leonard Online at
www.halleonard.com

I Won't Give Up

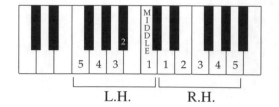

Words and Music by Jason Mraz
and Michael Natter

Relaxed

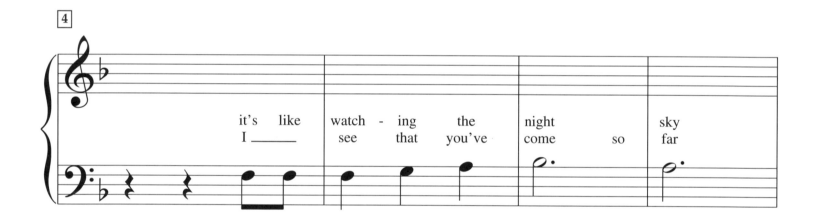

Duet Part (Student plays one octave higher than written.)

Relaxed

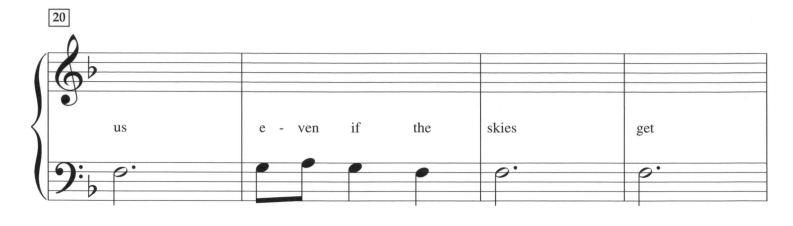

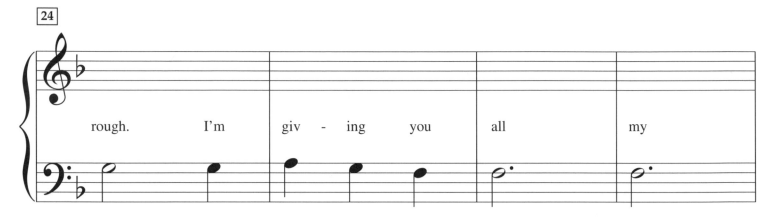

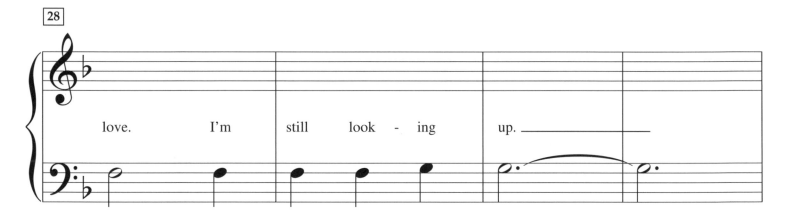

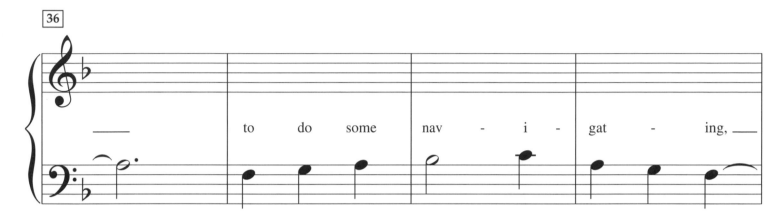

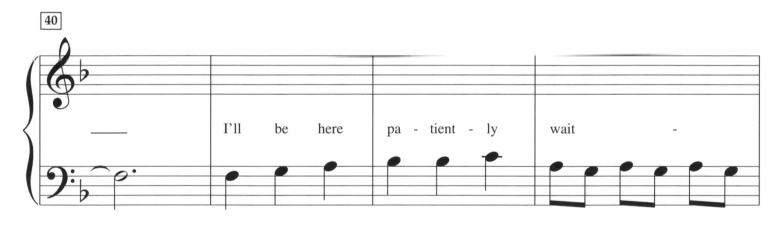

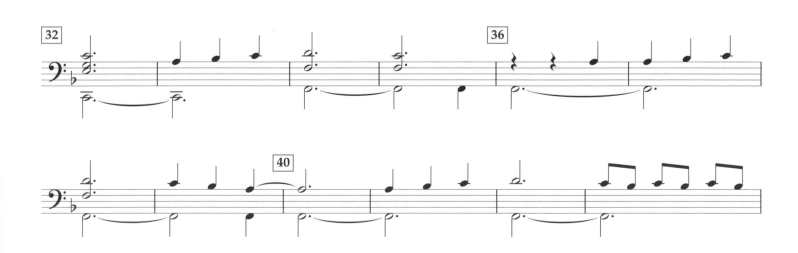

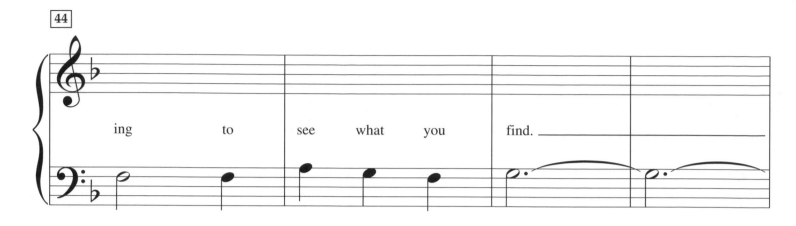

ing   to   see   what   you   find. _____

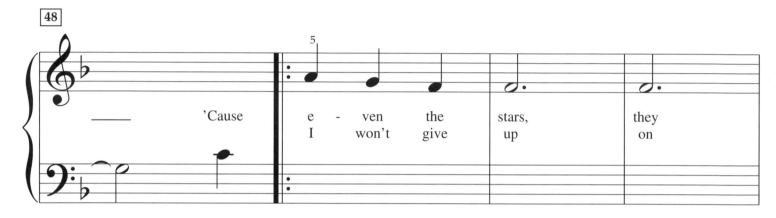

_____   'Cause   e - ven   the   stars,   they
            I   won't   give   up   on

burn,   some   e - ven   fall   to   the
us.   God   knows,   I'm   tough   e -

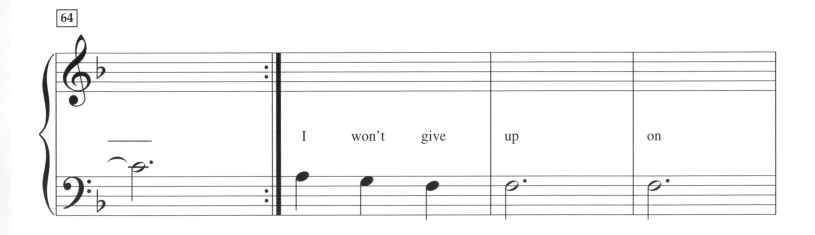

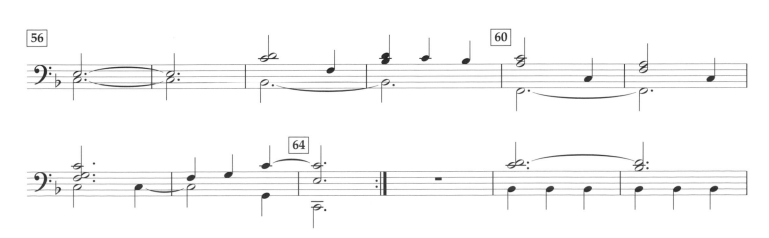

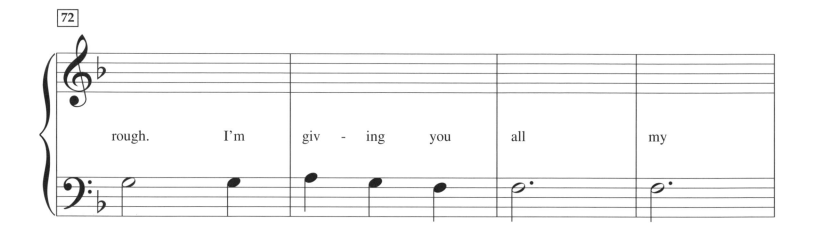

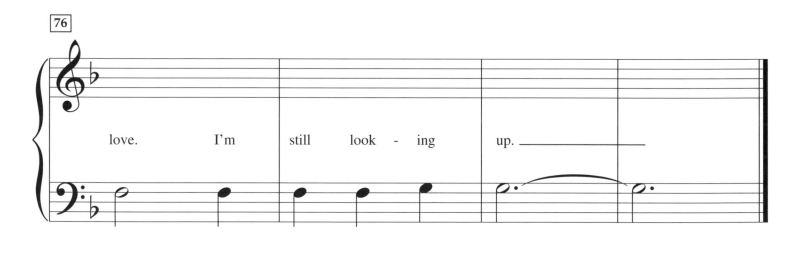

Cups

(When I'm Gone)

from the Motion Picture Soundtrack PITCH PERFECT

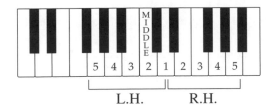

Words and Music by A.P. Carter,
Luisa Gerstein and Heloise Tunstall-Behrens

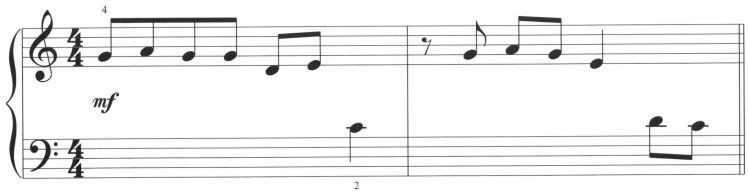

I got my tick - et for the long _____ way 'round _____

Duet Part (Student plays one octave higher than written.)

(clap)

two bottle o' whis-key for the way. And I sure would like some

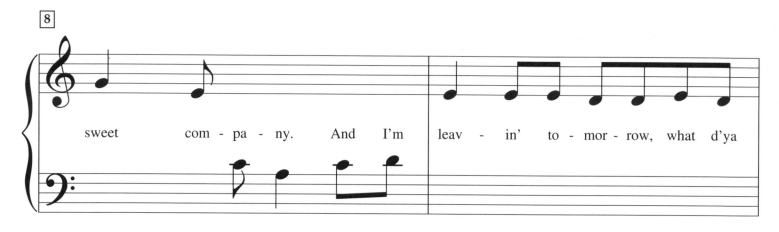

sweet com-pa-ny. And I'm leav-in' to-mor-row, what d'ya

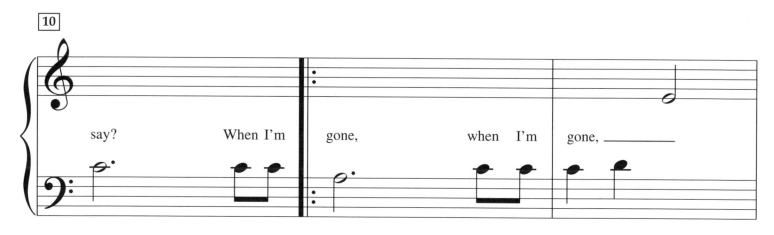

say? When I'm gone, when I'm gone, _____

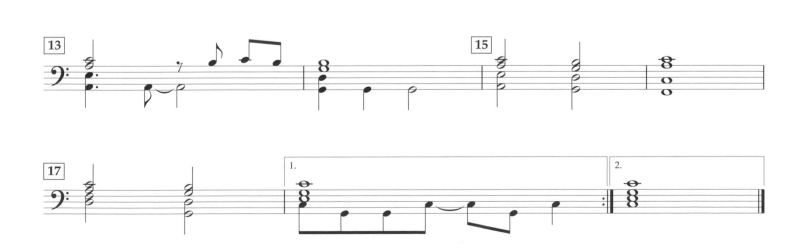

Home

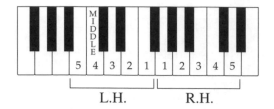

L.H.   R.H.

Words and Music by Greg Holden
and Drew Pearson

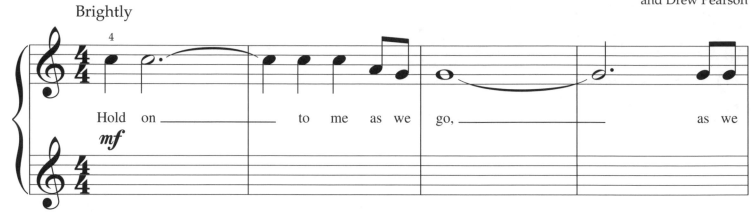

Brightly

Hold on _____ to me as we go, _____ as we

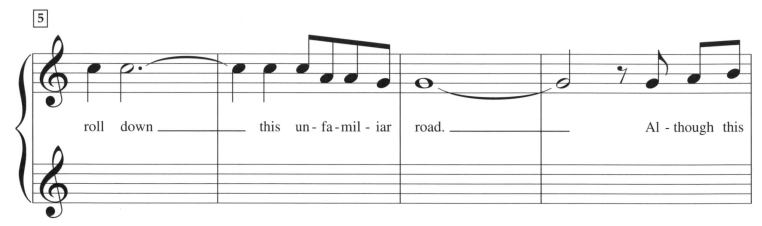

roll down _____ this un-fa-mil-iar road. _____ Al-though this

Duet Part (Student plays as written.)

Brightly

Skyfall
from the Motion Picture SKYFALL

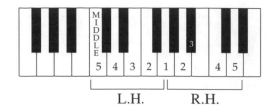

L.H.   R.H.

Words and Music by Adele Adkins
and Paul Epworth

Slow, mysterious

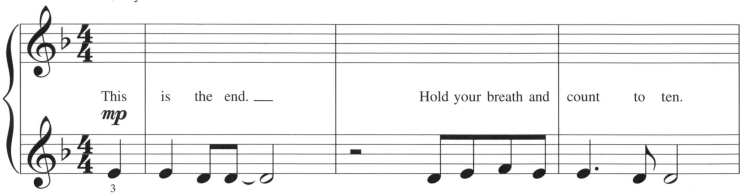

This is the end. ___ Hold your breath and count to ten.

Feel the earth move and then ___ hear my heart burst a-

Duet Part (Student plays one octave higher than written.)

Slow, mysterious

Love Story

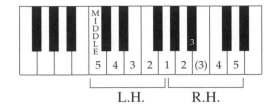

Words and Music by
Taylor Swift

Duet Part (Student plays one octave higher than written.)

Next To Me

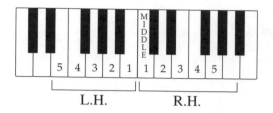

Words and Music by Emeli Sande,
Harry Craze, Hugo Chegwin
and Anup Paul

Driving

You won't find him drink-in' un-der ta - bles,
mon - ey's spent and all my friends have van - ished, and I can't

roll - in' dice and stay-in' out till three.
seem to find no help or love for free.

You won't ev - er find him bein' un-
I know there's no need for me to

Duet Part (Student plays one octave higher than written.)

Driving

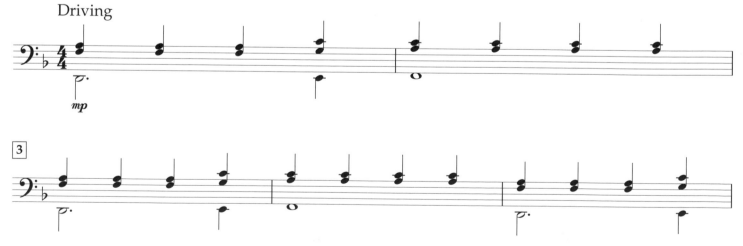

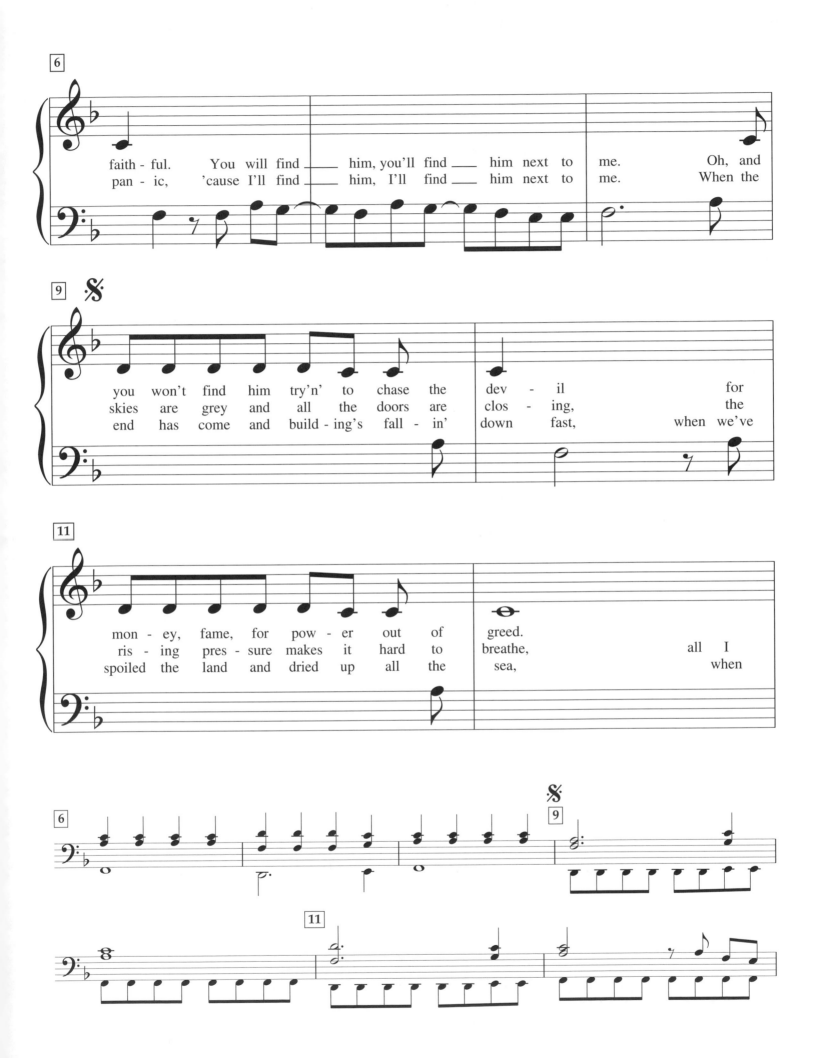

What Makes You Beautiful

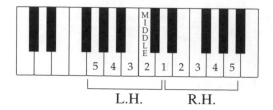

Words and Music by Savan Kotecha,
Rami Yacoub and Carl Falk

Moderately

You're in - se - cure, don't know what
So girl, c' - mon, you got it

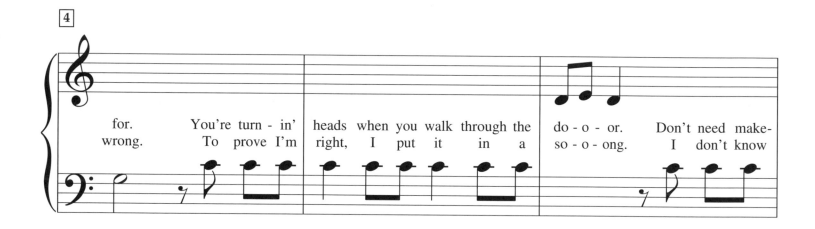

for. You're turn - in' heads when you walk through the do - o - or. Don't need make-
wrong. To prove I'm right, I put it in a so - o - ong. I don't know

Duet Part (Student plays one octave higher than written.)

Moderately

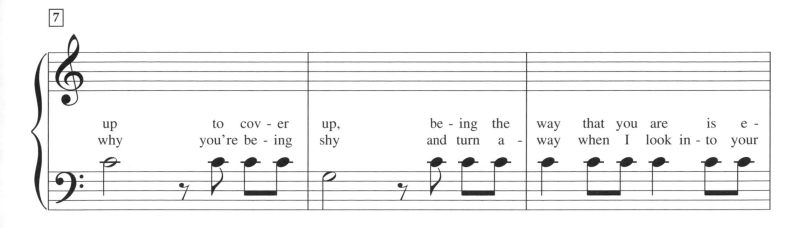

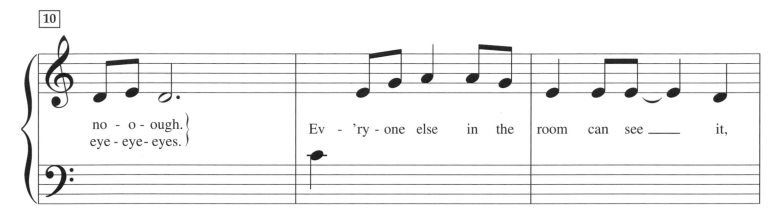

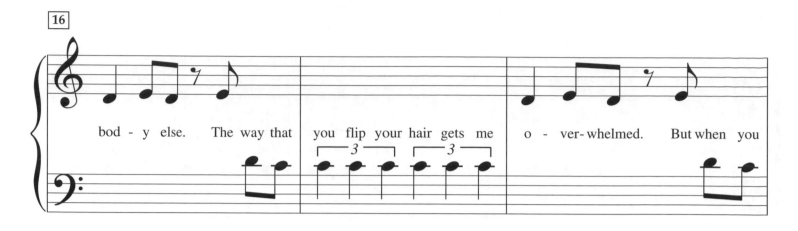

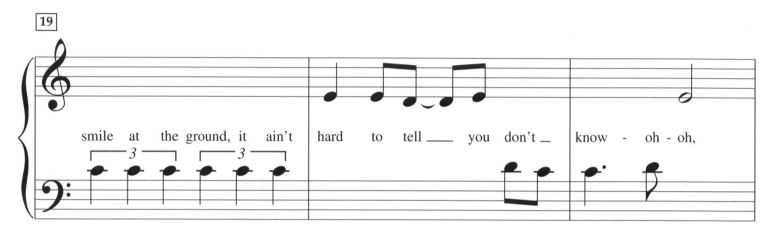

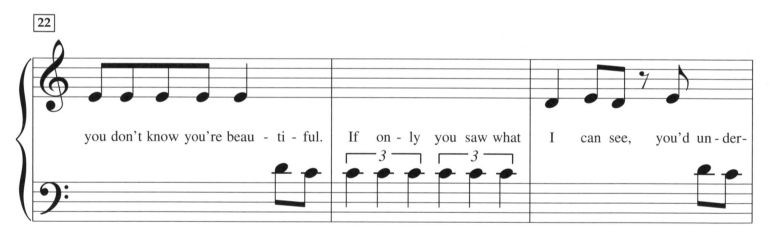

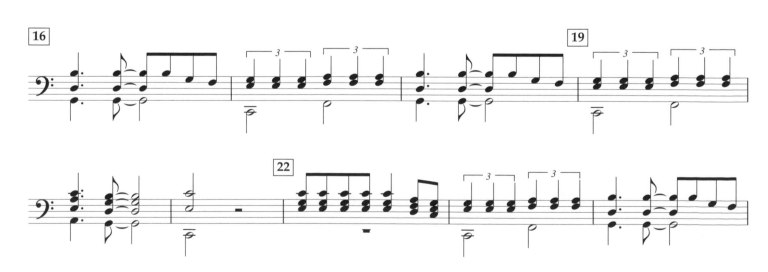

When I Was Your Man

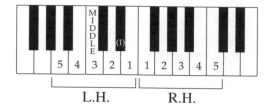

Words and Music by Bruno Mars,
Ari Levine, Philip Lawrence
and Andrew Wyatt

Same bed, but it feels just a lit-tle bit big-ger now. _____
My pride, my ___ e - go, my needs and my self - ish ways _____

Our song on the ra - di - o, but it don't sound the same. _____
caused a good strong wom - an like you to walk out my life. _____

Duet Part (Student plays one octave higher than written.)

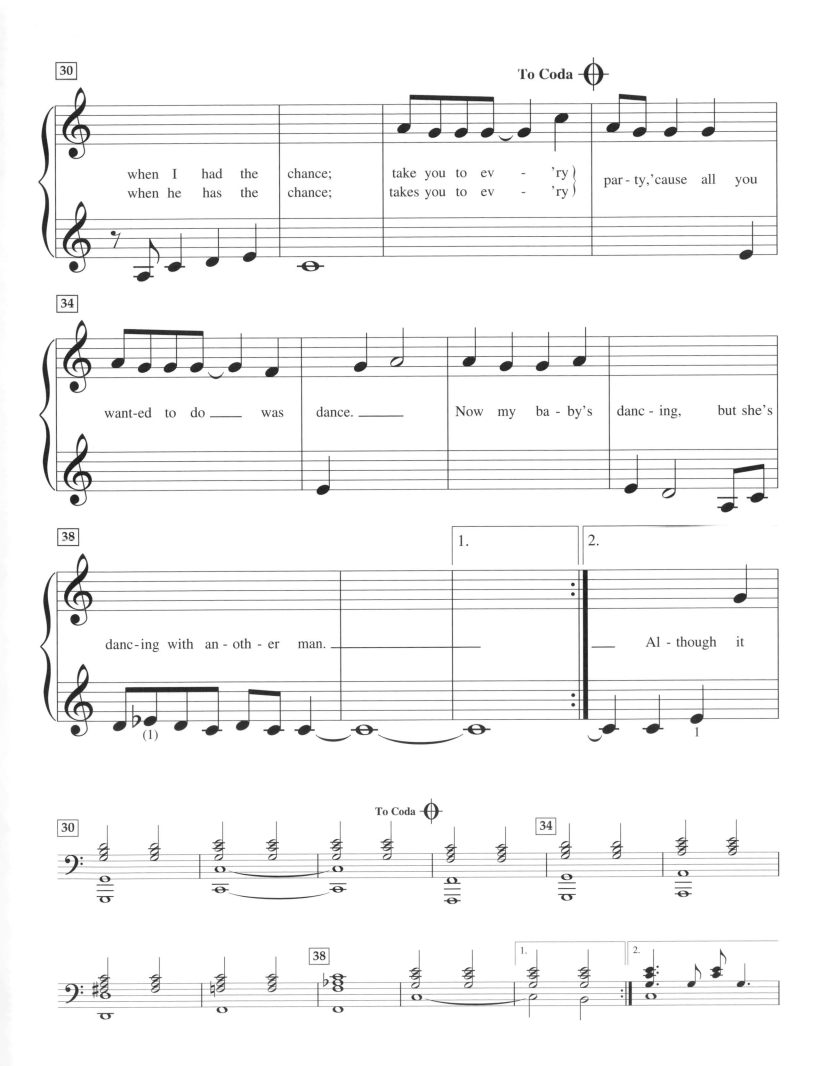

PLAYING PIANO HAS NEVER BEEN EASIER!

5-FINGER PIANO COLLECTIONS FROM HAL LEONARD

BEATLES! BEATLES!

8 classics, including: A Hard Day's Night • Hey Jude • Love Me Do • P.S. I Love You • Ticket to Ride • Twist and Shout • Yellow Submarine • Yesterday.
_____00292061...$8.99

CHILDREN'S TV FAVORITES

Themes from 8 Hit Shows

Five-finger arrangements of the themes for: Barney • Bob the Builder • Thomas the Tank Engine • Dragon Tales • PB&J Otter • SpongeBob SquarePants • Rugrats • Dora the Explorer.
_____00311208...$7.95

CHURCH SONGS FOR KIDS

Features five-finger arrangements of 15 sacred favorites, including: Amazing Grace • The B-I-B-L-E • Down in My Heart • Fairest Lord Jesus • Hallelu, Hallelujah! • I'm in the Lord's Army • Jesus Loves Me • Kum Ba Yah • My God Is So Great, So Strong and So Mighty • Oh, How I Love Jesus • Praise Him, All Ye Little Children • Zacchaeus • and more.
_____00310613... $7.95

CLASSICAL FAVORITES – 2ND EDITION

arr. Carol Klose

Includes 12 beloved classical pieces from Bach, Bizet, Haydn, Grieg and other great composers: Bridal Chorus • Hallelujah! • He Shall Feed His Flock • Largo • Minuet in G • Morning • Rondeau • Surprise Symphony • To a Wild Rose • Toreador Song.
_____00310611... $7.95

CONTEMPORARY MOVIE HITS – 2ND EDITION

7 favorite songs from hit films: Go the Distance (Hercules) • My Heart Will Go On (Titanic) • When You Believe (The Prince of Egypt) • You'll Be in My Heart (Tarzan™) • You've Got a Friend in Me (Toy Story and Toy Story II) • more.
_____00310687...$7.95

DISNEY MOVIE FUN

8 classics, including: Beauty and the Beast • When You Wish Upon a Star • Whistle While You Work • and more.
_____00292067.. $7.95

DISNEY TUNES

Includes: Can You Feel the Love Tonight? • Chim Chim Cher-ee • Go the Distance • It's a Small World • Supercalifragilisticexpialidocious • Under the Sea • You've Got a Friend in Me • Zero to Hero.
_____00310375...................................... $7.95

SELECTIONS FROM DISNEY'S PRINCESS COLLECTION VOL. 1

7 songs sung by Disney heroines – with a full-color illustration of each! Includes: Colors of the Wind • A Dream Is a Wish Your Heart Makes • I Wonder • Just Around the Riverbend • Part of Your World • Something There • A Whole New World.
_____00310847 ....$7.95

EENSY WEENSY SPIDER & OTHER NURSERY RHYME FAVORITES

Includes 11 rhyming tunes kids love: Hickory Dickory Dock • Humpty Dumpty • Hush, Little Baby • Jack and Jill • Little Jack Horner • Mary Had a Little Lamb • Peter, Peter Pumpkin Eater • Pop Goes the Weasel • Tom, Tom, the Piper's Son • more.
_____00310465.......................... $7.95

GOD BLESS AMERICA®

8 Patriotic and Inspirational Songs

Features 8 patriotic favorites anyone can play: America, the Beautiful • Battle Hymn of the Republic • God Bless America • My Country, 'Tis of Thee (America) • The Star Spangled Banner • This Is My Country • This Land Is Your Land • You're a Grand Old Flag.
_____00310828... $7.95

MOVIE MAGIC – 2ND EDITION

Seven gems from the silver screen arranged for beginners. Includes: Chariots of Fire • (Everything I Do) I Do It for You • Heart and Soul • I Will Always Love You • The Rainbow Connection • Summer Nights • Unchained Melody.
_____00310261 .... $7.95

THE SOUND OF MUSIC

8 big-note arrangements of popular songs from this perennial favorite musical, including: Climb Ev'ry Mountain • Do-Re-Mi • Edelweiss • The Lonely Goatherd • My Favorite Things • Sixteen Going on Seventeen • So Long, Farewell • The Sound of Music.
_____00310249..$9.99

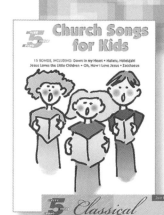

HAL•LEONARD® CORPORATION

7777 W. BLUEMOUND RD. P.O. BOX 13819 MILWAUKEE, WI 53213

www.halleonard.com

Disney characters and artwork © Disney Enterprises, Inc.